**BRILLIANT
WRITING
TIPS FOR
STUDENTS**

POCKET STUDY SKILLS

Series Editor: **Kate Williams**, *Oxford Brookes University, UK*
Illustrations by Sallie Godwin

For the time-pushed student, the *Pocket Study Skills* pack a lot of advice into a little book. Each guide focuses on a single crucial aspect of study giving you step-by-step guidance, handy tips and clear advice on how to approach the important areas which will continually be at the core of your studies.

Published

14 Days to Exam Success
Blogs, Wikis, Podcasts and More
Brilliant Writing Tips for Students
Completing Your PhD
Doing Research
Getting Critical
Planning Your Essay
Planning Your PhD
Reading and Making Notes
Referencing and Understanding Plagiarism
Reflective Writing
Report Writing
Science Study Skills
Studying with Dyslexia
Success in Groupwork
Time Management
Writing for University

**Pocket Study Skills
Series Standing Order
ISBN 978–0230–21605–1
(outside North America only)

You can receive future titles in this series as they are published by placing a standing order. Please contact your bookseller or, in case of difficulty, write to us at the address below with your name and address, the title of the series and the ISBN quoted above.

Customer Services Department, Macmillan Distribution Ltd, Houndmills, Basingstoke, Hampshire RG21 6XS, England

POCKET STUDY SKILLS

Julia Copus

BRILLIANT WRITING TIPS FOR STUDENTS

palgrave
macmillan

First published 2009 by
PALGRAVE MACMILLAN

Palgrave Macmillan in the UK is an imprint of Macmillan Publishers Limited, registered in England, company number 785998, of Houndmills, Basingstoke, Hampshire RG21 6XS.

Palgrave Macmillan in the US is a division of St Martin's Press LLC, 175 Fifth Avenue, New York, NY 10010.

Palgrave Macmillan is the global academic imprint of the above companies and has companies and representatives throughout the world.

Palgrave® and Macmillan® are registered trademarks in the United States, the United Kingdom, Europe and other countries

ISBN-13: 978-0-230-22002-7   paperback
ISBN-10: 0-230-22002-9   paperback

This book is printed on paper suitable for recycling and made from fully managed and sustained forest sources. Logging, pulping and manufacturing processes are expected to conform to the environmental regulations of the country of origin.

A catalogue record for this book is available from the British Library.

10 9 8 7 6 5 4
19 18 17 16 15 14 13

Printed in China

Contents

Acknowledgements   vi
Introduction   vii

Part 1 Punctuation   1

1 Full stop or comma? (avoiding
   the dreaded 'comma splice')   1
2 The comma (,)   5
3 The colon (:)   16
4 The semicolon (;)   25
5 The apostrophe (')   30

Part 2 Sentence structure   39

6 What makes a sentence a
   sentence?   39
7 The secret of clear sentences   46

Part 3 Paragraph structure   51

8 How to build a paragraph   51

9 The topic sentence   57

Part 4 Style   63

10 Maintaining clarity in longer
   sentences   63
11 Parallel sentence structure   74
12 Placing key points at the end
   of a sentence   76
13 Beware of overusing abstract
   nouns   81
14 Can I use 'I' in my essays?   86

Part 5 At a glance   93

15 How to improve your writing
   style – a checklist   93
16 Useful phrases for essay writing   96

Index   99

Acknowledgements

My thanks to Kate Williams for her encouragement and helpful comments, and t
Andrew Stevenson for his love and support, as well as his judicious eye. I am gratefu
also to my colleagues for many helpful and thought-provoking discussions – to th
English Department at Exeter University and to my fellow Fellows at the Royal Literar
Fund, who help students with their writing in universities across the country. A bi
thanks too to the students from many different disciplines who came to visit me a
Exeter for advice on their writing, whose challenging queries taught me to think in ne
ways about how writing skills should be communicated, and who have kindly allowe
me to use extracts from their essays.

Finally, I would like to thank Sallie Godwin, whose delightful illustrations not on
enhance the look of this book, but add so much to the explanations it contains.

Introduction

Clear writing is inextricably linked to clear thinking: the very process of trying to put complex ideas into the plainest possible words helps to clarify those ideas and generally sharpen up your powers of reasoning. It follows, therefore, that if you make the effort to improve the clarity of your writing, you'll automatically refine your ideas in the process!

The idea for this book came from my work as a writing adviser at Exeter University. I found that my students were confused by the conventional rulebooks I had on my shelves. It was a mixture of sympathy and shared frustration that led me to try out new ways of explaining various points of punctuation, grammar, style and essay structure. More often than not, I turned to visual images. *Think of the apostrophe as an arrow… Imagine the colon as the two curled fists of a speaker, ready to open as they offer an explanation to a statement they've just made.* Encouraged by how helpful the students found these explanations, I started to think about introducing them to a wider readership.

While working on this project, I focused on the fact that most students don't have time to wade through lengthy chapters on how to write the perfect essay. What they really want is solid and succinct guidance on their *most common* writing concerns – and tutors' most common gripes. Here is a book that meets that demand.

Why am I finding it hard to adjust to writing at university level?

First, it's important to realise that *you are not alone!* Students often complain about a big jump in tutors' expectations between school and university. In addition, many students feel under pressure to sound 'academic', and as a result, their writing style often becomes unnecessarily convoluted. This book will guide you, step by step, towards a clearer writing style.

What makes this guide different?

Simplicity: What you won't find here is pages of un-necessarily complicated rules and exceptions to rules. For instance, Chapter 5 introduces you to a simple rule for using the possessive apostrophe. Learn this one piece of advice, and you'll know all you'll ever need to know about the possessive apostrophe. That's because it's a rule that works in all instances – for singulars, plurals, compound words, nouns ending in 's', and all other types of words.

Easily memorable tips based on visual descriptions: There is a visual aspect to many of the tips in this book and, for that reason, many of them are accompanied b

Illustrations. It's often this visual aspect that makes the advice stick, since most people find it easier to remember pictures than they do ideas.

Up-to-date examples from student writing: Where appropriate, the writing tips are accompanied by common errors and problem sentences collected from students' own writing. These are followed by simple, step-by-step guidance on how to put things right, and suggested rewrites.

Additional help at the editing stage: No matter how good the advice is, nobody is going to express themselves perfectly first time round. At the end of each chapter, therefore, you will find a proofreading section, aimed at helping you polish up your essay after you've finished writing.

At a glance: There is also a handy 'at a glance' section at the end of the book, which includes a checklist of tips on how to improve your writing style, and a list of useful phrases for essay writing.

Pocket-size: Finally, as you'll have noticed, this book is small enough to carry with you at all times, in a pocket or bag, so that you can dip into it as and when you need. I trust it will prove a sturdy and dependable friend – during your years at university, and well beyond!

Julia Copus

Please note that, throughout the book, awkward or incorrect sentences are indicated by a cross, and problem-free sentences by a tick.

For Debs
with love and admiration

PUNCTUATION

1

Full stop or comma?
(avoiding the dreaded 'comma splice')

> 📷
> **PICTURE IT**
> A comma between two sentences is like a rusty hinge: it just isn't strong enough to hold the sentences together.

Students often make the mistake of joining two sentences with a comma. Sometimes the misplaced comma is referred to as a 'comma splice', and the resulting muddle is known as a 'run-on sentence' – a sentence that extends or *runs on* beyond its natural life. Here's an example:

❌ *The structure of DNA was discovered by James Watson and Francis Crick in 1953, until then it was considered a simple molecule.*

Full stop or comma?   1

The easiest way to solve the problem is to split the joined sentences into two, like this:

✅ *The structure of DNA was discovered by James Watson and Francis Crick in 1953. Until then it was considered a simple molecule.*

(If you're unsure about what constitutes a sentence, please see Chapter 6.)

 The bottom line is that in formal and academic writing, you should never use a comma in place of a full stop.

You *will* see sentences joined by commas in novels and short stories – even in works of non-fiction – but you will be hard pushed to find them in published academic work.

Recognising the problem

Have a look at the following extracts, all taken from student essays. Which of them contain comma splices, and are therefore wrong?

1 *This proves that MacDonald wasn't downstairs wearing the shirt when the crime took place, forensic analysis will almost certainly support this theory.*
2 *Protein molecules are made up of lengths of amino acids, the shape and behaviour of a protein molecule depends on the exact sequence of those amino acids.*
3 *It is striking how little this consensus resonates with public opinion, typically at least 60% of respondents in opinion polls express anti-trade views.*

The answer is that all the examples are wrong, because they all contain two main clauses – clauses that could stand as sentences in their own right.

Solving the problem

1 As we have seen, the simplest solution is to split the two parts into separate sentences, like this:

✅ *This proves that MacDonald wasn't downstairs wearing the shirt when the crime took place. Forensic analysis will almost certainly support this theory.*

You could in fact solve all instances of 'comma splice' in this way. Splitting spliced sentences in two will always solve the problem in grammatical terms, but may not be the best decision in terms of style.

2 If there is a continuity of thought between the two statements, a semicolon might be a better option:

✅ *Protein molecules are made up of lengths of amino acids; the shape and behaviour of a protein molecule depends on the exact sequence of those amino acids.*

> ❗ But beware … semicolons should be used sparingly, and until you feel absolutely confident about using them, it's probably best to divide your sentences with a full stop instead.

See Chapter 4 for more information on how to use semicolons.

3 Sometimes, the second statement explains or illustrates the first. In such instances a colon may be used:

✅ *It is striking how little this consensus resonates with public opinion: typically, a least 60% of respondents in opinion polls express anti-trade views.*

Chapter 3 explains how to use colons.

4 The final solution is to join the main clauses with a conjunction (such as 'and', 'but', 'so', 'yet', 'for' and so on) after a comma:

✅ *Many language theories have attempted to explain how children accomplish the incredible feat of learning a language from scratch, but it is doubtful whether any of these theories can fully account for the language acquisition capacity of the human infant.*

Proofreading for comma splices

Don't rely on the grammar checking facility on your computer to detect this problem such programs don't always pick up on comma splices. Instead …

1 Read through each questionable sentence and ask yourself, 'Would the clauses on either side of the comma make sense on their own as separate sentences?'
2 If the answer is yes, then they shouldn't be joined by a comma.
3 Use one of the four solutions outlined in this chapter.

2 The comma (,)

Many students seem to be unsure about where commas should – and, just as importantly, should *not* – be used. As a result, some people tend to overuse them, while others play safe and leave them out completely. The aim of this chapter is to put you at your ease, so that you feel you can use the comma with confidence where it is needed, and see at a glance where it is not.

Guidelines for comma use are reassuringly simple, and the logic behind those guidelines is simpler still. But before we begin, if you were told as a youngster to use a comma wherever you would pause or take a breath, the most useful thing you can do for yourself now is to erase that advice from your memory. Although it has some historical basis in fact, it is perhaps the single least helpful way to think about commas. It is also responsible for almost all of the misplaced commas seen in student writing.

The point of commas is to help guide your reader through a sentence, marking off clauses and sub-clauses along the way. In so doing, commas add clarity, grace and precision to your writing.

The origin of 'comma'

The word 'comma' comes from the Greek, κόμμα, meaning 'a piece cut off'. Unsurprisingly, then, a comma is used to mark off separate elements within a sentence.

PICTURE IT

It might be useful to picture the comma as a hook that hooks back or marks off separate parts within a sentence.

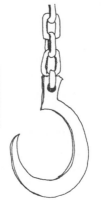

Five main uses of the comma

1 To separate items in a list.
2 To join main clauses that contain a conjunction ('and', 'but', 'or', 'so' etc.).
3 To mark off a phrase at the beginning or end of a sentence.
4 To mark off a phrase in the middle of a sentence.
5 To introduce a quotation (in certain instances).

To separate words or phrases in a list

he chances are you already feel fairly comfortable with this first use. If you're unsure,
heck to see if you can replace the comma with the word 'and' or 'or'. If you can, then
's in the right place. Here are some examples:

 The fruits I find easiest to eat are bananas, apples, grapes and satsumas.

 Potatoes can be mashed, sautéed, creamed, fried, baked or boiled.

ou could rewrite these sentences as follows: 'The fruits I find easiest to eat are ba-
anas *and* apples *and* grapes *and* satsumas' and 'Potatoes can be mashed *or* sautéed
r creamed *or* fried *or* baked *or* boiled.' The sentences would sound rather childlike,
ut technically speaking they would still be grammatically correct.

ometimes a list consists of whole clauses, rather than single words:

 *Andrew came home from work, made a cup of tea, took his shoes off, and started
 reading the paper.*

To join main clauses that contain 'and', 'but', or 'so' etc.

lace the comma immediately before the joining word, like this:

 *It rained all day on Saturday**, but** we decided to go to the seaside anyway.*

 *The lecture finished early**, so** we went into town.*

Commas aren't always essential in such sentences – especially when the two linked segments are short – but they are never wrong, and sometimes the meaning is completely altered if the comma is left out. Look at the following sentence, about a student who's been cooped up in a lecture hall all morning:

❌ *I breathed a sigh of relief as soon as the clock struck one and walked out into the sunshine.*

As it stands, the sentence suggests that the clock walked out into the sunshine, rather than the student. Inserting a comma in the right place removes any ambiguity:

✅ *I breathed a sigh of relief as soon as the clock struck one**, and** walked out into the sunshine.*

3   a. To mark off an introductory word, phrase or clause

Introductory words and phrases should be marked off from the rest of the sentence by a comma:

✅ ***However,*** *many other studies have suggested that children are not simply imitating adult speech.*

✅ ***At the same time,*** *the attraction of The Beatles went way beyond straightforward sex appeal.*

2 ***In order to fund state provision of certain goods and services,*** *it is necessary for the government to raise revenue through taxation.*

Used in this way, the comma may mark off a single word (as in the first example), a short phrase (as in the second), or a whole clause (as in the last example), but the principle is the same in every case. Introductory clauses often tell us how, when, why or where the main action happened. For instance, the sentence, 'After the war, a great many women lost their jobs', tells us *when* a great many women lost their jobs. Even so, such clauses are always surplus to requirements in grammatical terms. In other words, if they were removed, the rest of the sentence would still make sense.

Careful use of the comma to mark off an introductory phrase can sometimes prevent serious confusion:

> *Finally opening up her sister, Sarah realised that she'd been keeping quite a lot bottled up inside.*
>
> *Finally opening up, her sister, Sarah, realised that she'd been keeping quite a lot bottled up inside.*

The first sentence paints a gory picture of dissection. The second is a touching portrait of self-expression.

3 b. To mark off a word, phrase or clause at the end of the sentence

Concluding words and phrases are marked off from the rest of the sentence in exactl the same way:

✅ *There are many good arguments for staying on in education**, it has to be said.***

✅ *We arranged to meet at 'The Flying Aubergine'**, which is open all day on Sunda***

Again, the important thing is that the additional information is *non-essential* in gram matical terms. In the second example, the 'which' clause adds to the meaning, but th sentence would still make sense if we removed it.

4 To bracket off a word or phrase in the middle of a sentence ('paired commas')

A piece of non-essential information inserted into the middle of a sentence, almost lik an aside, is marked off by a pair of commas like this:

✅ *David**, who went to university in Manchester,*** *recently qualified as a psychc therapist.*

Remember to place a comma *on both sides* of the additional bit of information. Th commas work in exactly the same way as a pair of brackets would. In other word you were to remove the piece of additional information, to lift it cleanly away like a slice of cake, the remaining words should still make perfect sense.

After reading each sentence in the following table, try reading it again, without the middle section:

1st part of sentence	non-essential additional information (between commas)	2nd part of sentence
The NHS	*, set up 59 years ago,*	still focuses very much on treatment rather than prevention.
Pro-life groups	*, such as the Society for the Protection of Unborn Children,*	argue that life begins at conception.
Puberty	*, which usually starts between the ages of 9 and 16,*	can be a confusing time for many young people.

In each case, if we remove the bits between the commas, the sentence remains grammatically unharmed.

5 To introduce a quotation

Use a comma to introduce a quotation after an introductory clause or dialogue tag. (A dialogue tag is a statement that tells us who is speaking.) Here are some examples:

✅ ***As Wilson states,*** *'A tidy office will always give rise to the tidiest ideas'.*

✅ ***According to Stevenson,*** *'Drama is not highly regarded within the school curriculum'.*

But if the quotation follows on naturally from your own words, no punctuation is needed to mark it off from the rest of the sentence:

✅ *The 1947 Companies Act provided shareholders with a chance to 'improve the knowledge of their company's affairs' (Jones, 1977).*

Quotations that follow and support a complete sentence should be marked off by a colon rather than a comma.

✅ *Wordsworth maintains that loss of visionary power begins as soon as we are born: 'Our birth is but a sleep and a forgetting'.*

See Chapter 3 for more information on how to use colons to introduce quotations.

The three most common errors in comma usage

Joining two separate sentences together with a comma

❌ *Protein molecules are made up of lengths of amino acids, the shape and behaviour of a protein molecule depends on the exact sequence of these amino acids.*

This error, sometimes referred to as 'a comma splice', comes out high on the list of tutors' pet hates, and is dealt with in some detail in the previous chapter.

Forgetting to include the second comma after additional information in the middle of a sentence

❌ *My parents' computer, which they bought 20 years ago is seriously out of date.*

✅ *My parents' computer, which they bought 20 years ago, is seriously out of date.*

Without a closing comma after the word 'ago', the middle section has no end; it seems to leak into the rest of the sentence. The chances are you would never forget to insert a closing bracket where it's needed, because it would just look odd. Remember that a pair of commas acts in precisely the same way.

Separating the subject of a sentence from the verb it governs

This is a simple case of inserting a comma where it just isn't needed. Have a look at these extracts from student essays:

❌ *The health sector's main focus, should be shifted away from prevention and towards care.*

> ❌ *Adam Smith's work on the causes of the wealth of nations, has led economi*
> *thought for over two hundred years.*

A subject and verb should never be separated by a comma in this way – and i
makes no difference how long the subject is. Look again at that last example. Th
subject of the sentence is 'Adam Smith's work on the causes of the wealth of na
tions'. That whole phrase goes hand in hand with the main verb – 'has led' – an
when you place a comma between the two, the flow of the sentence is disrupted.
(If you are unsure about subjects and main verbs, see Chapter 6.)

Understanding the logic behind commas should help you to knock this bad habit o
the head. Just remember that the word comma originally means 'a piece cut off'. Th
one thing you don't want to do is to cut off or separate the subject of a sentence from
its verb.

Comma chameleon

It should be clear by now that commas are capable of
completely altering the meaning of a sentence. Here
are some more examples to prove the point. In each
pair, (a) is the more sensible option, but both make grammatical sense:

a *Having fallen over his pet goat, Toby needed stitches in his knee.*
b *Having fallen over, his pet goat, Toby, needed stitches in his knee.*

a *In the end there was no need to cook a big supper, as my boyfriend phoned to explain that he had eaten, himself, earlier in the day.*

b *In the end there was no need to cook a big supper, as my boyfriend phoned to explain that he had eaten himself earlier in the day.*

a *Taxi-drivers who suffer from road rage are putting their customers at risk.*

b *Taxi-drivers, who suffer from road rage, are putting their customers at risk.*

Proofreading for commas

❑ Read through your essay, and stop at every comma. Check to see that you haven't joined two or more stand-alone sentences with a comma. If you have, replace the comma with a full stop or semicolon, or add a conjunction ('and', 'but', 'so' etc.) after the comma.

❑ If you are using commas to bracket off a word or phrase in the middle of a sentence, make sure you've remembered to include TWO commas. (Don't forget the closing one.)

❑ Check that you haven't cut off your subject from its main verb.

❑ Finally, check that you haven't overdone it. You should only use as many commas as are necessary to express yourself clearly and avoid confusion.

3 The colon (:)

In many ways, the colon is one of the most valuable pieces of punctuation that exists. Its main (and perhaps most useful) function is to introduce a piece of information that sheds light on a statement made in the first part of a sentence. When used for this purpose it can stand for whole phrases such as *by which I mean* or *let me clarify what I've just said*. As a result, it is capable of turning many a lengthy and awkward sentence into something elegant and succinct. It is also (you'll be pleased to hear) incredibly easy to master.

> **PICTURE IT** When people offer an explanation during conversation, they often stretch out their hands, palms upwards, towards the listener. Think of a colon as the two curled fists of a speaker, ready to open as they offer an explanation for a statement they've just made.

By the time you've read this chapter you should feel supremely confident about what colons are and how to use them. This is not to say that you should start littering your writing with them, willy-nilly! On the other hand, there's no reason at all to shy away from using this helpful piece of punctuation when it really is the most appropriate means of expressing what you want to say.

When should I use a colon?

You should use a colon after a complete statement to introduce something that explains, illustrates or reinforces that statement. This might be a list, a quotation or any other remark that in some way sheds light on the original statement. Think of a colon as shorthand for the following sorts of phrases:

- *by which I mean*
- *to illustrate*
- *let me clarify what I've just said*
- *namely*
- *for example*
- *and the reason that I think that is*

We can see how this works in practice in the following two examples. In the first, try inserting a phrase like 'and the reason that I think that is' in place of the colon. In the second example, something along the lines of 'and those were' or 'namely' would make sense in place of the colon.

1 *Girls are clearly more suited to schoolwork than boys: each year they do consistently better than boys in their end-of-year exams.*

2 *Several teams were promoted last season: Blackburn Rovers, Southampton and Manchester City.*

Initial statement	Prompt from your imagined audience	2nd part of sentence (a reply to your imagined audience)
Realistically, there are only three possible solutions to the problem of poverty:	*Go on – tell us what those solutions are.*	government intervention, third-sector intervention, or a combination of the two.
Adam Smith believed that the state had responsibility in four main areas:	*Go on – what were they?*	defence, justice, public works, and education.

| In many ways parties are more bother than they're worth: | *Go on – tell us how, exactly.* | they're expensive, everyone drinks too much, and next morning the house looks like a bombsite. |
| In the area of language acquisition, children are not mere passive recipients of their environments: | *Go on – explain what you mean by that.* | rather than simply imitating what they hear, they are actively engaged in constructing a new language, complete with its own rules. |

There are three important points to note from these examples:

- In each case, the initial statement leaves the audience expecting more. It's as if that imaginary audience is waiting for an extra bit of information which explains, clarifies or justifies the statement.

- In each case, the initial statement is a complete sentence in its own right. (Note that in the normal course of writing, *the colon is always preceded by a complete sentence*.)

- What comes *after* the colon, however, need not be a full sentence, as in the first two examples in the table. It could instead be a list of words or phrases (including a bullet-pointed or numbered list).

A colon can stand in place of a whole phrase

The following sentence is rather awkward, and difficult to read:

❌ *Disabilities in the foetus bring about another situation which often results in contro- versy, <u>raising the issue of whether</u> it is ethical to terminate a pregnancy when the child is handicapped.*

Replacing the underlined phrase with a colon results in a more elegant and concise sentence:

✅ *Disabilities in the foetus bring about another situation which often results in contro- versy: is it ethical to terminate a pregnancy when the child is handicapped?*

To recap, a colon might be followed by any comment that sheds light on the original statement. In an essay, that illuminating comment is more than likely to be a quotation.

Using a colon to introduce a quotation

The good news is that there are no new rules to get to grips with for this type of colon usage: if you apply what you've learned up to this point, you'll find that you already know how to use the colon to introduce quotations! Just remember the following tip and you won't go far wrong:

 Use a colon only when the quotation is preceded by a complete sentence.

Here's an example of a quotation that follows a complete sentence:

> *Wordsworth's depiction of a kite can be seen as a metaphor for the Romantic audience's experience: 'The kite, in sultry calms from some high hill / Sent up, ascending thence till it was lost' ('The Prelude', line 242).*

If the quotation does *not* follow a complete sentence, punctuate as follows:

- *As Wall (2006) states, 'Good writing opens the doors of perception ... It informs and astonishes; shocks and delights.'*

  In this instance, a comma is used to mark off the introductory phrase <u>As Wall (2006) states ...</u>

- *Most educationalists now recognise that 'for many children, reading at home is simply not an option' (Stevenson, 2008).*

  In the second example, there is no introductory phrase. The quotation follows on naturally from the student's own words, so no punctuation is needed to mark it off from the rest of the sentence.

Special uses of the colon

It is worth noting, finally, that colons may also be used in the following instances:

▸ to juxtapose two contrasting statements, such as *Knowledge talks: wisdom listens* or *To err is human: to forgive, divine*. (Note that in such instances, the colon may be seen as shorthand for 'whereas'.)

▸ between two parts of a title – for instance, *Proofreading for clarity: a 4-step strategy*.

Two common errors in colon usage

1 Placing a colon in the middle of a sentence

❌ *The 1948 Act required that: every balance sheet and profit and loss account should show a 'true and fair view' of: the state of affairs and of the profit or loss of the company.*

Problem: The two misplaced colons clearly interrupt the flow of the sentence here. The writer seems to understand that colons are used to introduce information, but is unaware that they should be preceded by a complete sentence.

Solution: The easiest way to remedy the problem is to remove the colons altogether, like this:

The 1948 Act required that every balance sheet and profit and loss account should show a 'true and fair view' of the state of affairs and of the profit or loss of the company.

ere's another example of the same mistake:

Students taking part in the Duke of Edinburgh trip will need: a torch, a climbing helmet, safety goggles, walking boots, and a water bottle.

he fact that the writer is introducing a list here makes no difference. The colon still uts into the middle of the sentence. The best way to deal with the problem is to turn at introductory clause into a complete sentence:

Students taking part in the Duke of Edinburgh trip will need five essential items: a torch, a climbing helmet, safety goggles, walking boots, and a water bottle.

A colon should never interrupt a sentence

To summarise, a colon should never interrupt the flow of a sentence within the main body of your essay. This error is particularly common after certain expressions like *such as*, *which include*, *namely*, and so on.

An exception for bullet points... It is generally acceptable these days to introduce a bullet-pointed list with an incomplete sentence, especially after certain phrases. See Chapter 10 for more information on bullet points, and for examples.

2 Using a semicolon (;) in place of a colon

This is another very common error. It's important to remember …

 A colon is not interchangeable with a semicolon

Many students use semicolons where they should be using colons. On the one hand, this is not good news (because the semicolon and colon are used for quite different purposes), but on the other hand, it is the best *kind* of mistake you could make. If you are consistently using a semicolon every time you should use a colon, it follows that you understand how colons work! You have simply got into the habit of using the wrong punctuation mark. So if you are one of the many who make this particular error, take heart: it should be fairly straightforward to correct.

Proofreading for colons (in the main body of your writing)

☐ Is the colon preceded by a complete sentence?

☐ Does the colon introduce information that explains, illustrates, reinforces or in some other way illuminates a statement made in the first part of a sentence? *OR* …

☐ … if you are using a colon to juxtapose two contrasting statements (such as *Knowledge talks: wisdom listens*), could you replace the colon with the word 'whereas'?

The first thing you'll notice about this chapter is that it's nice and short. There is a reason for this: the semicolon is a stylish but *not essential* punctuation mark. Indeed, it's possible to turn out a perfectly good piece of writing without using semicolons at all. But that is not to say that they aren't useful.

The main function of the semicolon is to join two sentences that are closely related in meaning. A semicolon tells us that the sentence that's coming up is too closely linked to what has just been written to be divided from it by a full stop. From a grammatical point of view, a semicolon may always be replaced by a full stop without doing mischief to the overall sense of what is being said. What will have been lost in such cases is a certain nuance of meaning, as we shall see from the examples in the following pages.

SENTENCE	;	SENTENCE

Please note that, for the purposes of this chapter, the word 'sentence' is used in a loose sense to mean a group of words that could stand alone as a sentence in its own right.

Three main uses of the semicolon

1 To replace connecting words like 'and', 'but', 'so' etc.

✅ *We drove all night to make it to the campsite; when we got there it was full.*

That sentence might have been written like this:

✅ *We drove all night to make it to the campsite, but when we got there it was full.*

The semicolon replaces the word 'but', and *implies* the contrast between the tw
statements, rather than stating it outright.

Here are three more examples. Can you see which connecting word is being replace
in each instance? (See below for answers.)

a *The film had received some bad reviews; we decided not to go and see it after all.*
b *There were thousands of people at the march; every single one of them was carryin
   a banner.*
c *We'd already had quite a large lunch; that didn't stop us from going out for a slap-u
   meal in the evening.*

Answers: a = 'so'; b = 'and'; c = 'but'.

Note that in each case, a full stop could have been used in place of the semicolor
The semicolon signals to the reader that there is a continuity of thought between th
two sentences.

To join two clauses using a conjunctive adverb (*however*, *therefore*, etc.)

When words like *however*, *therefore*, *moreover*, *furthermore*, *nevertheless*, and so on begin a new main clause – a new complete thought – they must follow on from either a full stop or a semicolon, like this:

First main clause	;	Conjunctive adverb + ,	Second main clause
There are examples of individuals who would willingly work for free because they are passionate about their job	;	however,	such individuals are not in the majority.
The Sarbanes–Oxley Act applies to all companies that are listed on the US stock market	;	therefore,	even UK companies listed are subject to its regulations.
Many schoolchildren are intimidated by the exclusivity of certain older universities	;	consequently,	applications to such institutions are not as plentiful as they might be.

Remember to include a comma after the conjunctive adverb. Note, too, that all of the examples in the table could be written with a full stop instead of a semicolon, like this:

❷ *Many schoolchildren are intimidated by the exclusivity of certain older universities. Consequently, applications to such institutions are not as plentiful as they might be.*

The difference is that the semicolon signals to the reader that the two statements are closely connected in sense.

3 To separate items in a list – especially when those items already contain commas

Normally, items in a list are separated by commas. However, when you have a long complicated list that contains a lot of commas, the semicolon can be a useful way of avoiding comma chaos. Look at the following sentence:

> *Some of the guest lecturers teaching on this module are Earnest Gooding, a member of the Greener Planet Association, the originator of the popular Astronomy for Poets course, Frances Wright, and Gordon Wainwright, a leading researcher in this field.*

The problem is that commas have been used both to separate the different items in the list and to mark off bits of extra information *within* those items. But how many lecturers are listed here? If we tried to separate them, the list could look like this:

1 *Earnest Gooding*
2 *A member of the Greener Planet Association*
3 *The originator of the popular Astronomy for Poets course*
4 *Frances Wright*
5 *Gordon Wainwright, a leading researcher in this field*

Or it might look like this:

> *Earnest Gooding, a member of the Greener Planet Association*
> *The originator of the popular Astronomy for Poets course, Frances Wright*
> *Gordon Wainwright, a leading researcher in this field.*

Using semicolons between each item clears up the confusion:

> ✅ *Some of the guest lecturers teaching on this module are Earnest Gooding, a member of the Greener Planet Association; the originator of the popular Astronomy for Poets course, Frances Wright; and Gordon Wainwright, a leading researcher in this field.*

It now becomes clear that there are just three lecturers listed.

Proofreading for semicolons

You should be able to answer 'yes' to one of the first two questions:

☐ Are you using semicolons to separate items in a list? If not ...

☐ Do the two clauses on either side of the semicolon make complete sense on their own? In other words, could you put a full stop in place of the semicolon?

☐ Finally, check your essay for words like 'however' or 'therefore'. If they are used to start a new main clause (a new sentence, in effect), they must be preceded by either a semicolon or full stop.

5 The apostrophe (')

If you've ever wondered why we bother to use apostrophes at all, consider the following sentence, from which the all-important apostrophe has been removed:

Half way through the memorial concert, all the bands groupies were asked to leave, on account of their poor behaviour.

Is there only one band, or are there several? Does the 'all' refer to 'bands', or to 'groupies'? And who, exactly, has behaved badly – the band(s) or the groupies? Without the apostrophe, there is no way of knowing. Once we insert an apostrophe, however, the answers to these questions immediately become clear:

Half way through the memorial concert, all the band's groupies were asked to leave, on account of their poor behaviour.

We can see now that there is only one band, and that all of that band's groupies were asked to leave because of their own bad behaviour.

In this example, an apostrophe is needed to indicate possession – to let us know, in other words, who or what something belongs to. This is the area of apostrophe use that seems to cause most problems – though in fact, it's very easy to master.

BRILLIANT WRITING TIPS FOR STUDENTS

Apostrophe to indicate possession

Think of the possessive apostrophe as an arrow that points directly to the owner.

One of the main functions of the apostrophe is to tell us who or what something belongs to. Many students worry about where to put the apostrophe, but it's actually very simple. If you can remember the following rule, you can never go wrong:

 TOP TIP An apostrophe always comes DIRECTLY AFTER THE OWNER of the object, concept or thing.

The student′s overdue essay

This rule works in all instances – for singulars, plurals, compound words, nouns ending in –s, and all other types of words. You just need to work out who or what the owner is, and then put the apostrophe directly after it.

Picture the apostrophe as an arrow

Consider the following sentence (from which the apostrophe has been removed):

I must remember to return Mr Marshs poetry book.

First ask yourself, 'Who does the poetry book belong to?' Clearly, it belongs to Mr Marsh. The apostrophe therefore comes *directly after* 'Mr Marsh'. Try to visualise an arrow pointing towards the owner: 'Mr Marsh's poetry book'.

How does this work in practice?

The following table explains why the apostrophe belongs where it does:

Example sentence	Explanation
<u>*Mr Rochester's*</u> *ruin was perhaps inevitable.*	The apostrophe comes directly after *Mr Rochester* to show that the ruin belongs to Mr Rochester.
<u>*Tim and Rachel's*</u> *dog is extremely friendly.*	The apostrophe comes directly after *Tim and Rachel* to show that the dog belongs to Tim and Rachel.
My <u>*mother-in-law's*</u> *house is always spotless.*	The apostrophe comes after the whole phrase *mother-in-law* to show that the house belongs to the mother-in-law.

Example sentence	Explanation
Women's roles changed dramatically during this period.	The apostrophe comes directly after the word _women_ to show that the roles belong to the women.
All three _patients'_ queries were dealt with promptly.	The apostrophe comes directly after the word _patients_ to show that the queries belong to the patients.
Unfortunately, the _patient's_ appointment had to be cancelled, but she was able to reschedule for the following day.	The apostrophe comes directly after the word _patient_ to show that the appointment belongs to the patient.

❗ No apostrophe for _yours, hers, theirs, ours_

Students sometimes ask whether possessive pronouns ending in –s (like _yours, hers, theirs, ours_) should contain an apostrophe. The answer is no – not under any circumstances. The confusion arises from the fact that these words indicate possession. That is true, but if you apply the _Who-does-the-object-belong-to?_ test, you'll see that an apostrophe would only make sense if the object belonged to 'your' or 'her'!

What's the difference between *it's* and *its*?

It's easy to see why people get confused with this, but all you really need to know is that *it's* (with an apostrophe) always stands for 'it is' or 'it has'. Once you know this rule, you can apply it to any sentence.

 Read out your sentence using the words 'it has' or 'it is' in place of 'its/it's'. Does it still make sense?

'Yes' If it does, then you need to use an apostrophe.

'No' If not, then there should be no apostrophe.

Look at the following examples:

1 The dog is back in its kennel. (… *back in 'it has' kennel? … back in 'it is' kennel?* Clearly not! So, no apostrophe.)
2 It's been great to see you again. (*It has been great* …)
3 It's always raining these days. (*It is always* …)

Acronyms and dates

If you get to grips with the advice on the preceding pages, you will know pretty much all you'll ever need to know about the use of the apostrophe. However, for those of you who like to have all angles covered, here are two final tips on apostrophe use:

1 *Plurals of acronyms do not need an apostrophe:*
- **CDs** (Compact Discs)
- **UFOs** (Unidentified Flying Objects)
- **VIPs** (Very Important Persons)
- **FAQs** (Frequently Asked Questions)

2 *Dates do not need an apostrophe:*
- **1960s**

  … unless you abbreviate them by missing out the century, in which case you use an apostrophe to indicate the missing numbers
- **during the '70s and '80s** (where *'70s* stands for *1970s*)

An apostrophe that is wrongly inserted before the 's' of a plural noun is known as a 'greengrocer's apostrophe'. It is very common on handwritten – and even printed – signs on public display.

Proofreading for possessive apostrophes: a customised approach

If you know you have a problem with apostrophes, you should take some time to check specifically for them once you've finished writing your essay. Choose one of the following two methods:

Method 1: If you tend to use apostrophes where they're not needed, underline every apostrophe and ask whether you can justify its use. (Is it there to show that letters are missing? Does it denote possession? If not, remove it.)

Method 2: If you tend to miss out apostrophes, check every word ending in –s and ask whether the word denotes possession. If so, it needs an apostrophe. (But be careful with *its/it's*: remember that *it's* with an apostrophe always stands for 'it is' or 'it has'. Also bear in mind that there's no apostrophe in *yours, hers, theirs* and *ours.*)

Apostrophe to indicate missing letters

As well as denoting possession, apostrophes are used to show that letters are missing from a word. In this instance, you simply insert an apostrophe in the place where the missing letter or letters would have been, as in the following examples:

Example sentence	Explanation
I can't come until after the exams are finished.	can't = 'can not'. The apostrophe shows where the missing 'no' would go.
You're the last person I would have expected to see here.	You're = 'You are'. The apostrophe shows where the missing 'a' would go.

But please note that contractions like these are not usually acceptable in academic writing in any case.

6

What makes a sentence a sentence?

Like a one-man band, a sentence must be entirely self-reliant.

Just as a one-man band makes music without the help of other musicians, a sentence must make sense *all by itself*, without the help of neighbouring sentences. To take the analogy further, in the same way that a one-man band always contains a mouth organ and a drum, the two fundamental things that a standard sentence must never be without are a subject and a finite verb.

1 MAN Band

> **Note:** simply beginning a group of words with a capital letter and ending with a full stop isn't enough to make a sentence.

Take heart, though: if you have ever had work handed back to you with 'incomplete sentence' scrawled in the margin, you can comfort yourself with the fact that this is surprisingly common problem – even among students studying English! The information in this section will help you conquer the problem once and for all.

Two essential ingredients: a subject and a finite verb

What is a subject?

The subject of a sentence tells us what the sentence is about. It answers the question 'Who or what is performing the action of the sentence?'

What is a finite verb?

The finite verb relates directly to the subject. It is what makes the subject come to life, in that it tells us what that subject is doing (or has done or will do). It shows tense (past/present/future), and it changes its form to match the subject in number (singular or plural) and in person (I/you/he/she/it/we/they).

Recognising subjects and finite verbs

In the following sentences, I have underlined both the subject and the finite verb:

- *A laissez-faire economist* [subject] *would disapprove* [finite verb] of *state intervention in all but the most necessary of cases*.

- *Trace evidence at the scene of the crime* [subject] *includes* [finite verb] *footprints, soil samples, paint fragments and blood splatters*.

- *DNA* [subject] *is* [finite verb] *the main constituent of chromosomes*.

What other types of verbs are there?

There are other verbs – known as non-finite verbs – that do not go hand in hand with the subject of the sentence, and always stay in the same form. These fall into three groups:

- present participles, which end in '-ing' (*deciding, varying, feeling, being*)
- past participles (*decided, varied, felt, been*)
- infinitives (*to decide, to vary, to feel, to be*)

A sentence may contain any mixture of these additional types of verbs. The important thing is that it should contain at least one *finite* verb – a verb that tells us what the subject is doing.

The Standard Sentence Tester

☐ **Read for sense:** Read the 'sentence' out loud. Does it express a *complete* thought or action? Does it make sense in isolation? If you are at all unsure, go on to the next step.

☐ **Check for a subject:** Ask yourself, 'Who, or what, is performing the action of this sentence?' This is the subject. If you can't find one, you're in trouble: what you've written is not a proper sentence. If you can locate a subject, go on to the next step.

☐ **Check for a finite verb:** Does the would-be sentence contain a finite verb that tells us what the subject is doing?

(Bear in mind that there may be more than one subject and more than one finite verb.)

Punctuating the end of a sentence

The most important thing to signal to the reader is where one sentence ends and th next begins, and the commonest way to do this is with a full stop. A sentence may als end with a question mark or an exclamation mark (though you will rarely, if ever, nee to use an exclamation mark in the course of writing an essay).

How to avoid writing in sentence fragments

What is a sentence fragment?

A 'sentence fragment' is just another name for an incomplete sentence – a sentence that doesn't make sense by itself because it lacks either a subject or a finite verb. A good number of sentence fragments are in fact tail ends of sentences that have become detached from the main clause, like this:

❸ *The final band in the line-up was a group called The Raucous Racoons.* <u>*Which nobody had ever heard of.*</u>

Recognising sentence fragments

Some of the following examples are complete sentences and some are fragments. Can you see which are which? (Answers below.)

a *Emphasising the fact that more resources are needed.*
b *Many of these activities put additional strains on government spending.*
c *To ensure that safety procedures are put into place across the board.*
d *Cases such as these show the many levels and complexities of the abortion debate.*
e *For instance, rape victims, young mothers, and mothers at risk.*

Answers: b and d are complete sentences; a, c and e are sentence fragments.

Rewriting sentence fragments

The following sentence fragments have been rewritten as whole sentences. For clarity's sake, I have underlined the changes made to the original fragments.

❌ *The reason being a simple one: healthcare affects every one of us, whether we're nineteen or ninety.*

✅ *The reason is a simple one: healthcare affects every one of us, whether we're nineteen or ninety.*

❌ *Which requires the provision of a professional army paid for entirely by the State.*

✅ *This course of action requires the provision of a professional army paid for entirely by the State.*

❌ *To illustrate just one of the many ways in which art may enrich our lives.*

✅ *This benefit illustrates just one of the many ways in which art may enrich our lives.*

Proofreading for sentence fragments

If you read your work out loud, the chances are that you will be able to hear straight away whether what you have written is a full sentence or just a fragment. If you are uncertain, use the *Standard Sentence Tester* (see p. 42) to check that the phrase contains both a subject and a finite verb, and expresses a complete action or thought.

TOP TIP As well as reading your work out loud, it helps if you imagine each sentence in isolation. If you wrote the sentence up on a wall, would it make sense by itself?

What makes a sentence a sentence? 45

What your reader really wants to know is, 'Who dunnit? And what did they do?' The sooner you give them that information, the clearer your sentences will be.

Readers look for two bits of information when they read a sentence:

1 Who or what is the sentence about? (SUBJECT)
2 What is the subject doing? (MAIN VERB)

If you provide that information quickly and clearly, your sentences will be easy to understand. If, on the other hand, you ask your readers to work too hard (by taking a long time to get to the subject, for instance) the chances are you'll end up confusing them. And that is the very

Who dunnit?

last thing you want to do – especially if one of the readers in question is your tutor, with a whole pile of other essays to mark.

> **TOP TIP** A sentence becomes instantly clearer if you start with the subject and get to the main verb quickly.

The following two rules of thumb are particularly useful if you're struggling with sentence clarity:

Start with the subject

The subject tells us what the sentence is about. Sentences that take a long time to get round to the subject can therefore be difficult to understand:

> *By being able to identify human voices from as early as twelve hours after birth, <u>babies</u> are perceptive to the sounds of human language from very early on.*

The whole thing becomes far clearer if we start with the subject:

> ✓ *<u>Babies</u> can identify human voices from as early as twelve hours after birth, and this makes them perceptive to the sounds of human language from very early on.*

Adding a short introductory phrase: Very often, you will want to begin a sentence with a short introductory phrase or word, but the aim should still be to introduce the subject as soon as possible. Such a phrase is simply marked off from the rest of the sentence by a comma, and the subject follows immediately afterwards, as can be seen from the example on the following page.

☑ *On the other hand, <u>babies</u> can identify human voices from as early as twelve hours after birth, and this makes them perceptive to the sounds of human language from very early on.*

2 Keep the subject and the main verb close together

A long gap between the subject and the main verb can also lead to confusion:

☒ *<u>Some students</u>, simply because they feel the need to sound 'academic', <u>write</u> unnecessarily complicated sentences.*

☑ *<u>Some students</u> <u>write</u> unnecessarily complicated sentences, simply because they feel the need to sound 'academic'.*

Recognising the problem

Many sentences lack clarity either because they introduce their subjects too late, or because there are too many words separating the subject from the main verb. Read the following sentence out loud and try to identify the cause of the problem. (See below for answer.)

☒ *Human life, though many people feel it begins later in pregnancy when the foetus takes on a more human look, properly begins at conception.*

Answer: In this particular sentence, there is too long an interruption between the subject and the main verb.

Rewriting unclear sentences

The revised version introduces the subject nice and early, and then gets to the main verb quickly. Note that the additional information has been moved to the end of the sentence, but the sentence still ends on a strong note:

> *Human life* properly *begins* at conception, though many people feel it begins later in pregnancy when the foetus takes on a more human look.

Proofreading for sentence clarity: a 4-step strategy

Reading your work out loud, sentence by sentence, is the best way to hear whether or not it makes sense. Each time you come across a sentence that sounds unclear to you, highlight it. Then follow this simple 4-step strategy:

1 Find the subject and the main verb and underline them.
2 Ask yourself if the subject is introduced early enough in the sentence.
3 Ask yourself if the subject and main verb are close enough together.
4 If the answer to 2 or 3 is 'No', then rewrite as necessary.

It's hard to imagine any long piece of writing – a story, an essay, a novel – with no paragraphs at all. It would certainly be very difficult to read – a dense, unbroken block of text, with no visual cues to suggest where the reader's gaze might rest or their mind pause for a moment before changing direction.

So what is the point of paragraphs? Paragraphs are there to organise ideas into manageable chunks. When we write in paragraphs we're helping readers negotiate their way through our thoughts. We begin a new paragraph whenever we want to change gear – whether that be to introduce a new point, to contrast sides in a debate, or to convey any other kind of shift in thought or emphasis.

In terms of essay writing, well-structured paragraphs guard against chaos. It might help to think of paragraphs as drawers in which you place closely related objects. If you clutter up the drawers with lots of other, random objects (tennis balls and textbooks in the sock drawer, for instance), it soon becomes very difficult to find things! In other words, paragraphs stop your argument from sprawling out of control.

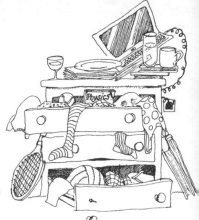

Paragraph content

Every paragraph should …

1 *have a clear central point*

Often that main point is expressed in the opening sentence, or 'topic sentence'.

2 *be uniform in subject matter*

Each paragraph should have just one, clear focus.

3 *contain only relevant information*

Don't make the mistake of thinking that the more facts you put in the more the marks you'll get. *All* the material in your paragraph should be there to support or illustrate your main point.

A simple formula for paragraph structure

The template below illustrates how you might go about constructing a standard paragraph.

Topic Sentence

Explain and clarify
the point you made in the topic sentence (in one to two sentences).

Evidence
Provide supporting evidence to back up your main point (quotations, statistics, examples, illustrations etc.).

TOP TIP
If you find your paragraph dividing naturally into smaller sub-sections, each needing its own supporting evidence, try creating separate paragraphs for each of those sub-sections.

Springboard comment/question:
In the final sentence you might want to comment on the evidence, or pose a question, in a way that leads the argument towards its next point. But please note that this last stage is not essential – and may not even be appropriate – for every paragraph, or in every type of essay.

Putting the formula into practice

The following paragraph is taken from an essay on abortion.

1 **Topic sentence**	Poverty is another major contributory factor in the rising rates of teenage abortions.
2 **Explain/clarify**	The majority of girls from England and Wales who get pregnant in their teens come from the poorest parts of the country.
3 **Evidence**	Figures from the *Office for National Statistics* suggest a direct link between a girl's poverty and the likelihood that she will have an abortion, which is not surprising in view of the fact that half of all pregnancies under 18 occur in the UK's most deprived wards. A recent article in *The Daily Telegraph* revealed that the London borough of Lambeth has the highest rate of teenage abortion in the UK, with one teenage girl in every 23 having had an abortion in 2006.
4 **Springboard comment/ question**	But do girls as young as 13 really have the maturity to understand the social, moral and emotional implications of abortion?

NB: The 'springboard comment' often goes instead at the start of the next paragraph

See the following chapter for a full explanation of how to write and use topic sentences

Links between paragraphs

Linking adjoining paragraphs establishes continuity and helps convey a sense of development in your argument. Look at any structured and coherent piece of writing and you'll probably find that each paragraph is clearly connected with the one that precedes it. On a basic level, transitions between paragraphs show the reader how your writing is moving from one main point to the next. Here are two useful techniques for establishing connections between your paragraphs:

Use linking words and phrases. You may want to use a single word (like *However,* …) or a short phrase (like *By the same token,* …). Such transitions act as signposts: they show the reader the route your argument is taking. In effect, they say (for example), 'OK, I've discussed that point. Now we're going to turn left to explore the alternative viewpoint.'

Pick up on key points and words. Reiterate a key point or repeat one or more of the key words from the previous paragraph – and then build on it.

Try to use both these techniques wherever you can.

> **Beware of relying too heavily on linking words and phrases alone**
> Remember that if there is no real connection between your paragraphs, no amount of elegant phrasing is going to disguise that fact.

Proofreading for paragraph clarity

For each paragraph in your essay, ask yourself:

☐ Does the paragraph stick to one clear central point?

☐ Can you sum up that central point in a few words?

☐ Is that main point clearly stated in the opening sentence? In other words, is there a topic sentence? (If the topic sentence appears later in the paragraph, try moving it to the start.)

☐ Is everything you've included in the paragraph *relevant* to the main point? Does it clarify or support it in some way? (If not, it doesn't belong there! Either move it to another paragraph, or remove it completely.)

☐ Is it immediately obvious how each new paragraph relates to the previous paragraph?

9 The topic sentence

> 📷 **PICTURE IT** A topic sentence is like a clothes peg from which the rest of the paragraph hangs.

he opening sentence of each para-
raph is often referred to as the 'topic
entence', because it announces the
verall topic of the paragraph. All the
nformation in the rest of the paragraph
xpands on, explains or elucidates
nat topic. In other words, the whole
aragraph depends on the opening topic sentence in much the same way as a piece
f clothing on the washing line depends on the peg from which it hangs!

What is the point of a topic sentence?

A topic sentence is there, as the name suggests, to introduce the topic, or subject of your paragraph, and to make a general point that will be explained, explored and illustrated in the rest of the paragraph. In many ways, therefore, it is the most important sentence in each paragraph. In fact, in a perfectly constructed essay, it should be possible to understand the main thrust of the argument by reading the topic sentences alone.

Put simply, topic sentences serve two main purposes. First, they let your reader know what to expect in the rest of the paragraph. Secondly, they help *you*, the writer, to stay focused on your argument as you write.

So how do I write a topic sentence?

The main thing to remember is …

 All topic sentences should have two parts to them:
1 The topic itself.
2 The main point (a statement about the topic).

The table on the following page shows how this works in practice.

1. Topic	2. Main point
The Behaviourist learning theory	reduces the child to a passive recipient of environmental stimuli.
The film *Annie Hall*	pokes fun at anti-Semitism by way of the main character's Jewish inferiority complex, his paranoia and his distrust of the opposite sex.

Sometimes the topic comes *after* the main point, like this:

1. Main point	2. Topic
There are several strong arguments for state intervention	in healthcare provision.
There are numerous advantages	to studying later in life.

The topic sentence tells us what to expect

In the first of these examples, for instance, we can guess that the paragraph will attempt to explain and justify the claim it makes, and provide examples that show precisely *how* the Behaviourist learning theory reduces the child to a passive recipient. Similarly, in the last example, we can be fairly sure that the rest of the paragraph will list and explore the advantages of studying later in life.

The case of the missing topic sentence

Look at the following paragraph, from which the opening sentence (the topic sentence) has been removed:

> ---
> -- There is a high
> correlation with a child and parent regarding height, weight, shape and form of
> features, body build and skin colour. Many dimensions of personality, such as
> temperament, also seem to be inherited (Wong 1999). Inherited potential is decided
> at conception as the genes from both father and mother combine to form the new
> individual.

Janet MacGregor, *Introduction to the Anatomy and Physiology of Children* (Routledge, 2000)

1 What is the overall subject, or topic, of the paragraph?
2 What general point (or points) is the author making about that subject?

Answers: The topic, as you may have guessed, is 'inherited characteristics', and the missing topic sentence (which appears on the following page) is a comment on the nature of such characteristics. It contains, as we would expect, two clear parts. First the topic itself is announced, and then a statement is made about that topic:

Inherited characteristics are transmitted from one generation to the next in a random way, and they strongly affect the end result of growth and the progress towards it.

If we look back now at the main body of the paragraph, we can see how this opening statement is clarified, illustrated and explored.

Over to you

The following process will help you to create topic sentences that are both carefully considered and clearly stated.

1 What is the general subject, or topic, of your paragraph?

....

2 What point do you want to make about that subject?

....

3 Now write your topic sentence in a single, declarative statement.

....

....

....

Proofreading for topic sentences

As well as inserting topic sentences as you write your essay, it is a good idea to check for them during the editing stage. As you read through the finished draft of your essay, ask yourself, *What is the central point of this paragraph?* If you find your answer in the opening sentence, all well and good. If the central point is buried deep in the middle of the paragraph, you may need to move that sentence to the beginning.

 If you find it impossible to locate the central point of your paragraph, the chances are that it needs rewriting altogether.

10 Maintaining clarity in longer sentences

Let's get one thing clear: there is nothing innately wrong with longer sentences. Although short sentences are often clearer (and clarity should always be your primary concern), varying the length of your sentences makes the overall rhythm of your writing more interesting, and the writing itself more enjoyable to read.

The problem arises when the sentence structure begins to slide out of shape. Long, rambling sentences that lose the reader along the way are often a sign of muddled thinking, and your writing will benefit greatly from any efforts you make to bring such sentences under control.

In fact, knowing how to control sentences is one of the most powerful tools available to you in your progress towards a clearer writing style. Your aim should be to help your readers navigate their way through your sentences with the minimum of effort. Remember that by taking the trouble to write more clearly, you will also be teaching yourself to *think* more clearly.

This section teaches you three helpful techniques for disentangling knotty syntax and maintaining clarity in longer sentences. But first we'll look at ways of ensuring that you can spot the problem in your own writing.

Recognising the problem

If you find it difficult to follow the line of argument within a single sentence, or if you can't get to the end of a sentence without taking a breath, then it almost certainly needs rewriting. There are two specific warning signs to watch out for:

1 **Strings of relative pronouns (*who, that, which*, etc.).** Some long sentences use a series of relative pronouns to tack on a series of extra clauses. The result is often awkward-sounding and difficult to read. Take a look at this example from a biology essay:

Example A: *The bases are stacked one on top of the other, which is vital for the stability of the molecule, though it is still a structure that can be broken apart in certain circumstances, which results in the DNA being denatured.*

Here's what that sentence looks like when broken down into parts:

The bases are stacked one on top of the other,
  → *<u>which</u> is vital for the stability of the molecule*
  → *though it is still a structure*
  → *<u>that</u> can be broken apart in certain circumstances,*
  → *<u>which</u> results in the DNA being denatured.*

2 **Strings of present participles (-*ing* words).** Another warning sign is long strings of words ending in -ing. Here's an example from a film student's essay:

Example B: *Brian disguises himself by preaching to a crowd of spectators, leading them to think that he is the Messiah, forcing him to criticise the Romans in order to convince the crowd that they are mistaken, causing him to be arrested, abandoned, and eventually sentenced to death.*

Broken down into its component parts, the sentence looks like this:

Brian disguises himself by preaching to a crowd of spectators,

→ *leading them to think that he is the Messiah,*

→ *forcing him to criticise the Romans*

→ *in order to convince the crowd that they are mistaken,*

→ *causing him to be arrested, abandoned, and eventually sentenced to death.*

Solving the problem

Here are three approaches you can take to tackle the problem of rambling sentences.

1 Break the sentence into smaller units

The simplest solution is to split the sentence into several shorter sentences. For instance, Example B might be rewritten like this:

> *Brian disguises himself by preaching to a crowd of spectators. This leads them to think that he is the Messiah. He is then forced to criticise the Romans in order to convince the crowd that they are mistaken. This in turn causes him to be arrested, abandoned, and eventually sentenced to death.*

There will be occasions when simply breaking your rambling sentence up into smaller units like this is enough. The revised version here is certainly easier to understand than the original, but the writing sounds choppy and disjointed, and too many of the revised sentences begin with 'This'. If breaking the sentence into smaller parts doesn't solve the problem entirely, you may also want to try the technique on the following page.

> **!** Watch out for long strings of *-ing* words or *who/that/which* clauses in your writing. They are usually a sign that your sentences are sprawling out of control and need rewriting.

2 Insert a recap word

This technique is not only easy to master, it will make your writing sound clear and stylish. Here's what to do:

▶ Think of a word that summarises the first part of the sentence – a 'recap' word.
▶ Insert the recap word, and continue with the rest of the sentence.

Let's see how the technique works with our two model sentences. The start of the first sentence originally looked like this:

> *The bases are stacked one on top of the other, which is vital for the stability of the molecule …*

First, we need to think of a recap word, a word that summarises the first part of the sentence. 'Arrangement' seems to be a good solution here, because it sums up the way in which 'the bases are stacked one on top of the other'. Now we're ready to rewrite:

> *The bases are stacked one on top of the other, <u>an arrangement</u> which is vital for the stability of the molecule.*

The revised sentence makes it absolutely clear what the 'which' refers to.

Now here's the original beginning of sentence 'B':

> *Brian disguises himself by preaching to a crowd of spectators, leading them to think that he is the Messiah …*

n this instance, a word like 'ruse' or 'deception' sums up the first part of the sentence.
‑he revised sentence might look like this:

> *Brian disguises himself by preaching to a crowd of spectators, <u>a ruse</u> that leads*
> *them to think that he is the Messiah.*

ractising the recap technique

s you'll see from the examples in the table below, this technique really comes into its
wn when the first part of the sentence is fairly long. Once you get into the habit of us-
ng recap words, the device should become an automatic part of your writing process.

First part of sentence	Recap word that summarises the information	Remainder of sentence
The new President of the Student Union made up her mind to ban all live music events in the run-up to exams …	*decision*	…, a decision that has proved controversial with many students.
The Royal National Lifeboat Institution rescues an average of 22 people each day from the seas around the UK and Ireland …	*service*	…, a service that is by no means cheap to deliver.

First part of sentence	Recap word that summarises the information	Remainder of sentence
It could be argued that up until recently the media has not accorded young women sufficient status within society …	*omission*	…, an omission that has prompted this group to step forward and make their mark on popular culture.

3 Repeat a key word and then continue

First get to a key word in your sentence, and stop:

Smith believed that the State should also be responsible for the provision of certain public <u>amenities</u>

Place a comma after the key word, and then repeat it:

Smith believed that the State should also be responsible for the provision of certain public <u>amenities, amenities</u>

Finally, add a relative pronoun (*who*, *that*, or *which* etc.), and continue the sentence:

… <u>amenities which</u>, if owned privately, might lie in poor condition.

Note how the repeated word allows the reader to breathe and to think, and makes it absolutely clear what the *who*, *that*, or *which* is referring to.

Using bullet points

Bullet points enable you to set out a series of related points in an uncluttered format. They can be a useful way of breaking up long, sprawling lists of information into more manageable chunks.

Take a look at the following example from an essay on forensics:

> *On arrival at the scene, efforts should be made to tape off the area and restrict access to necessary personnel, establish a route of entry, take notes from anyone who was present at the time of the crime, take measures to prevent contamination of evidence (for example, protective suits should be worn) and photograph the scene in detail (including position and condition of the bodies).*

Here is the same information again, presented as a list of bullet points

> *On arrival at the scene, efforts should be made to:*
> - *tape off the area*
> - *restrict access to necessary personnel*
> - *establish a route of entry*
> - *take notes from anyone who was present at the time of the crime*
> - *take measures to prevent contamination of evidence (for example, protective suits should be worn)*
> - *photograph the scene in detail (including position and condition of the bodies).*

Note how the space between each point encourages the reader to pause before moving on to the next piece of information, and as a result the brain is able to take in one unit of meaning at a time as the eye moves down the page.

> The use of bullet points in essays is frowned upon in some subject areas, while in many others (such as Business Studies, Economics and so on) it is welcomed. If you are at all unsure of the policy in your particular subject area, check first with your tutors.

Bullet points and stem statements

Remember that each point in your list should make sense when read with the stem statement. Here's the kind of thing you should try to avoid:

Past members of the university can use their Membership Card to benefit from:
- *lifetime membership of the University Library*
- *you can use the Sports Centre whenever you like*
- *many local businesses offer a discount*
- *access to the university's careers service.*

 Every point in a list should lead on naturally from the stem statement.

Try reading the middle two items directly after that opening statement. They simply don't make sense! In the following, revised version, each separate point reads as a natural completion of the first part of the sentence:

> Past members of the university can use their Membership Card to benefit from:
> ▸ *lifetime membership of the University Library*
> ▸ *full-time access to the Sports Centre*
> ▸ *special discounts at many local businesses*
> ▸ *access to the university's careers service.*

Please note that, ordinarily, you would never interrupt a sentence with a colon, but when using bullet points, that rule is relaxed.

In short

Using a mixture of the techniques in this chapter will help sharpen your syntax, clarify your argument, and generally make your work easier to read. The advice in the next chapter will ensure that, however long your sentence is, it will still make perfect grammatical sense …

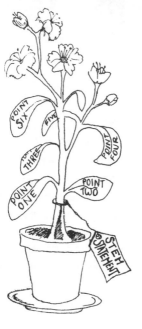

11   Parallel sentence structure

When there is a series of clauses in a sentence, the whole thing becomes easier to read if the clauses are parallel in structure. For instance, the following sentence sounds awkward:

❌ *Falstaff is portrayed as a lecherous man who sees the wives not only as sexual conquests but also able to enhance his wealth.*

But if we use a parallel structure, the readability improves immediately:

✅ *Falstaff is portrayed as a lecherous man who sees the wives <u>not only as</u> sexual conquests <u>but also as</u> a means of enhancing his wealth.*

In diagram form, the improved version looks like this:

Falstaff is portrayed as a lecherous man who sees the wives ⎯⎯⎯⎡   <u>**not only as**</u> *sexual conquests.*
                                              ⎣   <u>**but also as**</u> *a means of enhancing his wealth.*

We can see from the diagram that the two parts of the sentence are parallel with each other. The following table contains two further examples of jumbled sentence coordination, both taken from student essays. In each case, the awkward sentence appears first (in the shaded cells), and is followed by a suggested rewrite.

❌ First we need	to examine how this self-conscious style is achieved and then there is the motivation of the authors.
✅ First we need	<u>to examine</u> how this self-conscious style is achieved and then <u>to question</u> the motivation of the authors.
❌ The Spice Girls showed young women that they could use their feminine qualities	to get what they want, to do what they want and they no longer had to be oppressed by a male dominated culture.
✅ The Spice Girls showed young women that they could use their feminine qualities	<u>to get</u> what they want, <u>to do</u> what they want and <u>to break free</u> from the oppression of a male dominated culture.

Improving parallel structure in your own work

If a sentence sounds imbalanced, try writing it out in diagram form:

stem statement ——— **first part of sentence**
              └——— **second part of sentence**

Well-coordinated sentences will make your work a lot easier to read – and in the long run that means that your ideas will be easier to understand.

12 Placing key points at the end of a sentence

 TOP TIP The last few words of a sentence carry particular emphasis.

Students often lose valuable marks because their key points are difficult to see or to understand. In many cases that's because those key points are presented halfway through a sentence which then trails off into a series of secondary clauses and additional information, much as this sentence does! In order to land the necessary punch, your main idea needs to be placed instead at the *end* of the sentence.

Remember: the stress point of every sentence is located in the last few words. Instead of burying your ideas in the middle of sentences, the trick is to present them loudly and clearly in those dominant closing words.

The good news is that simply by swapping round the different bits of information in your sentence, you can ensure that your key ideas are never overlooked.

It might help to picture each sentence as a shape that is flared at one end – like a megaphone. If you want your writing to pack a punch, make sure your main points appear in the widest end of your sentences, where they will make the most noise.

Recognising the problem

Take a look at this extract from a film student's essay on the works of Eisenstein:

❸ *Eisenstein's ideas remain influential and relevant to film makers, however.*

Even though the sentence is relatively short, the main point is all but lost because of the way the sentence fades away at the end. The significant point here is that Eisenstein's ideas have *lasted* – that they remain important to film makers *to this day*.

Solving the problem

By moving the 'however' to the start of the sentence, the emphatic end point can be reserved for that all-important main idea:

☑ *However, Eisenstein's ideas remain influential and relevant to film makers **to this day***.

The revised sentence begins with the topic ('Eisenstein's ideas') and ends with the key point that's being made about that topic.

If there is non-essential additional information tagged on to the end of a sentence, and if that information is obscuring your main point, move it to the beginning of the sentence.

Rewriting to improve sentence emphasis

In each of the following examples, the key point appears in boldfaced type, so that you can see which words need to be repositioned. In the suggested revisions the key points are shifted to the end of the sentence, and as a result, the sense is greatly improved.

Original sentence	Suggested revision
The fact that the report **provided the first conceptual framework for UK financial reporting** makes it an important historical landmark.	What makes the report such an important historical landmark is the fact that it **provided the first conceptual framework for UK financial reporting**.
It appears that **right from birth** the human infant is equipped with the neural prerequisites for acquiring language, as postulated by the nativist theory.	As postulated by the nativist theory, it appears that the human infant is equipped with the neural prerequisites for acquiring language **right from birth.**
The new government **initially reduced the effects of the quasi-markets** as they moved into power.	As they moved into power, the new government **initially reduced the effects of the quasi-markets**.

Proofreading for sentence emphasis

Read through your work to check that your sentences end with the words you most want to emphasise. If you come across sentences that seem to peter out, here's what to do:

1 Ask yourself, 'What's the main point I want to get across?', and then underline that point.

2 Delete any redundant phrases that add nothing important to the overall meaning, but that have simply been tagged onto the end of the sentence as padding.

3 Place any non-essential additional information at the beginning of the sentence rather than at the end.

4 Place the main point in the last few words of the sentence.

Partly because of a perceived need to sound 'academic', many students are fond of using posh-sounding abstract nouns that tend to confuse what it is they are trying to say. In fact, the obscure nature of such words is precisely what makes them so appealing. Writing accurately can be hard work – and when you're pushed for time or don't know what it is you want to say it's very tempting to plump for a vague or abstract word that you hope will convey some sort of satisfactory meaning.

There is nothing wrong with using abstract nouns sparingly, and in the right places, but using them in the wrong places not only obscures meaning; it can also lead to some very cluttered syntax, as we shall see.

The advice in this section is based on the fact that many abstract nouns are formed from simple verbs and adjectives. They are easy to recognise, because they often end in *-tion*, *-ment*, *-ness*, *-ity*, *-ence*, and so on.

Words like *implication*, *pronouncement*, *disinterestedness*, *multiplicity*, *convergence* are all abstract nouns. In the next few pages you will learn a simple technique for converting such words back to the straightforward verbs and adjectives from which they came. If you use the technique, your writing will automatically become clearer and more direct.

The following table shows how a lot of abstract nouns are formed:

Abstract noun often used in an attempt to sound 'academic'	Verb or adjective from which the abstract noun was formed
implication	imply (verb)
pronouncement	pronounce (verb)
disinterestedness	disinterested (adjective)
convergence	converge (verb)
desirability	desirable (adjective)

Recognising abstract nouns

We now know how to recognise abstract nouns by their endings. Here is another pointer that will help you to spot abstract nouns in your own writing:

 Abstract nouns, of the type that cause problems in student writing, are very often followed by the word 'of'.

In the following example, the abstract noun has been underscored with a wavy line – and, as you might expect, it is followed by the word 'of':

❌ One subtle *indication* of this is shown in how Thatcher's power decreased towards the end of her final term.

By choosing to use an abstract noun instead of a verb, the writer has been forced to continue with some very awkward phrasing. The resulting sentence is over-complex, repeats itself, and is difficult to read. As soon as we change the abstract noun to a verb, the sentence immediately becomes easier to understand:

✅ This is subtly *indicated* by the way in which Thatcher's power decreased towards the end of her final term.

Being able to convert abstract nouns back to verbs and adjectives is the key to rewriting many cluttered sentences in a clearer, more direct style.

Rewriting sentences containing abstract nouns

In the next four examples, all taken from student essays, the abstract nouns are again underscored with a wavy line. The last of the sentences (d) is grammatically incorrect and none of them is easy to understand.

a Critical *uncertainty* remains as to the precise dating of the narrative sources.

b Whether the *motivations* for contributing by firms are the prospect of good publicity or a genuine desire to give back to the community remains debatable.

c One *requirement* of the new Act was for all companies to publish a sales figure in the Profit and Loss account.

d Joyce's *experimentation* with the idea of nationality in Ireland is multi-faceted, and in doing so he opens the subject up for further debate.

The revised versions replace the abstract noun with its root verb or adjective, and as a result they are far easier to understand:

a Critics remain *uncertain* about when precisely the narratives were written.

b Whether firms *are motivated* to contribute by the prospect of good publicity or by a genuine desire to give back to the community remains debatable.

c The new Act *required* that all companies should publish a sales figure in the Profit and Loss account.

d Joyce *experiments* with the idea of nationality in Ireland on many levels, and in doing so he opens the subject up for further debate.

Proofreading for abstract nouns

f you think you may be overusing abstract nouns in your own work, here's how to go
about correcting the problem:

1. First, identify any awkward-sounding sentences that contain abstract nouns. Remember to look out in particular for words that have the following endings:
   - *-tion*
   - *-ment*
   - *-ness*
   - *-ity*
   - *-ence/-ance*

2. If you think the abstract noun is responsible for tangling up your syntax, convert it back to its root verb or adjective.

3. Locate the subject of the sentence. Ask yourself, 'Who or what is performing the action of this sentence?' (For more information on subjects, see Chapter 6.)

4. Rewrite the awkward sentence starting with the subject, and using the original *verb* or *adjective* from which the abstract noun first came. This should be a fairly straightforward task: the syntax will tend to sort itself out, and you should find that it's far easier to write the revised sentence than it was to write the original.

14 Can I use 'I' in my essays?

Students often come to university with a mental checklist of rules about what is and is not permissible in essay writing – such as the much-quoted *Never use 'I'*. Since these 'rules' often derive from half-remembered or poorly understood advice from schooldays, it is not surprising that some of them are either over-simplistic or just plain wrong. When you need to make it clear to the reader that an opinion is your own, it is entirely appropriate to use the first person in an essay. In such cases – unless you are specifically told not to do so – you should go ahead and use it.

Personal opinion in essays

Behind the specific debate about use of the first person, there lurks a more general question: is it acceptable to voice personal opinions in an essay? Most assignments ask you to present a logical argument based on a series of connected ideas that are supported by evidence. If the ideas you present or the deductions you make during the course of your essay are your own, then why pretend otherwise?

> *The important thing – whether or not you use 'I' – is to back up any statements with appropriate evidence.*

Using 'I' – a quick checklist

Consider using 'I' if you can answer yes to any of the following:

☐ Are your efforts to avoid using 'I' tying your writing up in knots?

☐ Are you trying to indicate where your own opinion departs from those you have quoted?

☐ Are you writing a reflective essay or a presentation report?

In addition, be sure to check that the tutor who has set your assignment does not object to the use of 'I'.

Why would I want to use 'I' in an essay?

Using the first person in your essays has several advantages. It can allow you to:

▶ develop sound analytical skills by encouraging you to place your own thoughts alongside those of critics or other academics

▶ offer a unique perspective on your subject, and point out where your ideas depart from those already in print

▶ write with greater clarity.

Steadfastly avoiding 'I' can result in some very awkward phrasing, as can be seen from the following example:

❌ *Drawing on a range of supporting literature, the issue of to what extent the political views of the Romantic poets influenced those of the educated classes will be explored.*

✔ *Drawing on a range of supporting literature, I shall explore the extent to which the political views of the Romantic poets influenced those of the educated classes.*

Please note, also, that the use of 'I' is essential in reflective and self-reflexive essays as well as in presentation reports.

Are there times when using 'I' is not appropriate?

The short answer is yes!

- For instance, it's inappropriate to use 'I' when the emphasis is on the process rather than your own ideas, as is often the case in science subjects:

  ❌ *As I heated the solution in an evaporating basin, I noticed that it started to spit.*

- Nor should you use 'I' simply to state a fact:

  ❌ *I think that Harriet Jacob's slave narrative presents us with a wide array of vivid characters, including the tyrannical slave-master, Mr. Flint.*

Unless you wish to set yourself up as a dissenting voice among the academics you're quoting, that initial 'I think that' is unnecessary.

- Lastly, avoid using 'I' when how you formulated an opinion is neither interesting nor relevant:

  ❌ *I noticed, as I read through Adam Smith's 'Wealth of the Nations', that he has a preference for minimal government intervention.*

  ✅ *In 'Wealth of the Nations', Adam Smith states a preference for minimal government intervention.*

It's partly a question of phrasing

An academic essay is not the place to air opinions based solely on personal taste or experience. If you feel nervous about using the first person, you might want to steer clear of the following types of phrases, which lend themselves to the expression of such opinions:

I think that …   I believe that …   I feel that …   I like or *dislike …   I prefer …*

Verbs that refer to the processes of arguing and explaining are a safer bet:

argue   demonstrate   show   explain   suggest   prove

Here's an example, taken from the introduction to an essay on poverty:

✓ *Ultimately, then, state intervention alone is an inadequate solution to the problem of poverty in the UK, as I intend to demonstrate.*

As this example suggests, using the first person is especially useful in the introduction to an essay, where you are setting out the main points in your argument, and showing the reader where you stand in relation to the material you're quoting.

To summarise

Unless told otherwise, it's fine to use 'I' when you are analysing or commenting on material, and when the emphasis is on personal deduction rather than process. Tutors do want to know your ideas, but they also want you to make use of what academics have said about the subject. You can satisfy those demands by ensuring that you always place your own ideas in context.

Remember: protocol varies from subject to subject and in the final event, if you are at all uncertain, check with your tutor.

How to improve your writing style – a checklist

☐ **READ YOUR WORK OUT LOUD.** This is easily the best way to detect glitches in your writing. Remember … *The ear will hear what the eye does not see.*

☐ **USE ROLE-PLAY.** If you have trouble getting an idea down onto paper, it can help to imagine that you are trying to get your point across to a child – an intelligent child, but one who knows very little about your subject – and use this as the basis for your written explanation. Confused writing is often the result of confused thinking, and the effort of trying to make yourself understood vocally may be all that's needed to clarify your writing.

☐ **STICK TO THE FAMILIAR.** Avoid using complex-sounding words (especially words you don't understand!) purely in an attempt to sound 'academic'. Many tutors say that one of their worst nightmares is an essay full of thesaurus substitutions.

☐ **BE CONCISE.**

1 Cut out meaningless words (*sort of*, *actually*, *basically* and so on).

2 Cut out words that repeat the meaning of other words, such as …

past history	*true facts*	*revert back*	*completely eliminate*
period of time	*final outcome*	*small in size*	*basic fundamentals*
brief in duration	*close proximity*	*join together*	*estimated at about*

3 Avoid long-windedness. In many instances, whole phrases can be replaced by a word or two. Why say 'exhibiting behaviour of a riotous nature' when you mean 'being disruptive'? Here are some common examples to watch out for:

due to the fact that = because	*concerning the matter of = about*
in the event that = if	*carry out an analysis of = analyse*
at this moment in time = now	*until such a time as = until*

☐ **VARY RECURRING WORDS AND PHRASES** – especially when quoting or para-phrasing. Use the following list to help you:

[Academic X] *points out*, *says*, *states*, *claims*, *suggests*, *proposes*, *puts forward the idea*, *shows*, *demonstrates*, *indicates*, *maintains*, *argues*, *counters* – and so on.

☐ **BEWARE OF MISUSING IDENTICAL-SOUNDING WORDS.**

Here are some common examples:

there = *in that place*

they're = *they are*

their = *belonging to them*

affect = *have an influence on*

effect = *bring about*

principle = *a firm belief; a scientific law*

principal = *chief, main; the head of a school, college or university*

☐ **AVOID CONTRACTIONS.** (*you're*, *won't*, *didn't* and so on) in academic writing.

☐ **DON'T RELY ON YOUR COMPUTER'S GRAMMAR-CHECK FACILITY.**

Clever as it is, it doesn't get everything right!

16 Useful phrases for essay writing

To give an overview of content (in the introduction)
This essay deals with / aims to prove / considers / looks at …

To make a general point
By and large, …; Generally speaking, …; As a rule, …

To introduce an example
To illustrate, …; To illustrate this point …; Take for example …; [*Named text / scholar / situation*] … offers us numerous examples of …

To draw a conclusion from examples you've given
It is clear, therefore, that …; This evidence suggests that …

To pause and emphasise a main point
It is worth noting that …; It is worth stating at this point that …; That last example highlights the fact that …; We [*or* 'one'] might even go so far as to say that …

To restate a point
In other words, …; Put simply, …; In short, …; To put it another way, …

To introduce a new point
Turning now to the question of ...; Having considered ..., we are now in a position to ...

To introduce an exception to the rule
While it is generally agreed that ...; While it may be true that ...

To introduce a counter-argument or alternative viewpoint
However, it is important to remember that ...; Nevertheless, one should also consider that ...; All the same, it is likely/possible that ...; On the other hand, we could argue that ...; Another possibility is that ...

To introduce quotations
According to X, ...; As X points out, ...; In his book/paper/article on [*subject*] entitled [*title*], X makes the point that ...; X claims that ...; Writing in 1969, X argued that ...

To refer to research
It has been shown that ...; Certain academics such as [*X and Y*] point out that ...; Many academics argue that ...; Research has shown that ...; According to some academics/ experts ...; X states/argues/proposes/maintains/notes that ...

To follow quotations or research
This claim supports the idea that ...; It is clear, then, that ...; This evidence suggests that ...; We might conclude, therefore, that ...; This seems unlikely given the fact that ...; This argument does not take into account that ...

N.B. Always remember to name your sources when quoting research.

To draw a conclusion from your main points

From the arguments presented in this essay, one might conclude that ...; All of this points to the conclusion that ... / seems to confirm the idea that ...; To sum up, / summarise, / conclude, ...

Use this space to make a note of any other useful phrases you come across in the course of your own reading:

Index

abstract nouns, 81–5
  proofreading for overuse
    of, 85
  recognising, 81–3
  replacing, 84
'academic' writing style
  and contractions, 37, 95
  and personal opinion, 90
  and problems with diction
    and syntax, vii,
    81–2, 94
acronyms, punctuation of, 35
apostrophes, 30–7
  and acronyms, 35
  as arrows, 32
  and dates, 35
  golden rule, 31
  greengrocer's, 35
  to indicate missing letters,
    37
  to indicate possession, 31

  and possessive pronouns
    (*yours*, *hers* etc.), 33
  power to alter meaning, 30
  proofreading for, 36
argument
  counter-argument, 97
  and use of 'I', 88, 90
  using paragraphs
    to control
    development of, 52,
    53, 55
  using topic sentences to
    signpost, 58
  within a single sentence,
    65
awkward phrasing, *see*
  syntax

bullet points, 71–3

central points, *see* key
  points; paragraphs
cluttered writing style, *see*
  syntax
colons, 4, 12, 16–24
  common errors, 22–4
  confusion with semicolon,
    24
  to improve concision,
    16, 20
  to introduce quotations,
    12, 20–1
  proofreading for, 24
  special uses of, 22
commas, 5–15
  before *and*, *but*, *so* etc.,
    4, 7–8
  and breathing, 5
  'comma splice', 1–4
  common errors, 13–14

with conjunctive adverbs (*however*, *therefore* etc.), 27
to introduce quotations, 12, 21
main uses, 6
to mark off a concluding word or phrase, 10
to mark off an introductory word or phrase, 8–9, 47–8
origin of, 6
'paired' (parenthetical), 10–11
power to alter meaning, 9, 14–15
proofreading for, 15
purpose of, 5
to separate items in a list, 7, 28
computer grammar-check facility, 95
concision, 94
and colon use, 16, 20

conjunctions (*and*, *but*, *so* etc.)
after commas, 4, 7–8
how to replace with semicolon, 26
conjunctive adverbs (*however*, *therefore* etc.), 27, 29
contractions (*you're*, *won't*, *didn't* etc.)
and academic writing, 37, 95
punctuation of, 37

dates, punctuation of, 35
diction, *see* word choice

first person, *see* 'I', use in essays
flow (improving)
links between paragraphs, 55, 56
repeating key words, 70
using 'recap' words, 68–70

full stops, 2, 3, 40, 42

grammar-check facility, 95

homophones, 95
'however', 27, 29, 77

'I', use in essays, 86–91
and clarity, 88
inappropriate use of, 89
and personal opinion, 87, 88, 90, 91
in self-reflexive essays and reports, 88
ideas
how to emphasise, 76–80
refining of, vii
using 'I' to assert, 88, 90
using paragraphs to organise, 51–2
see also key points; paragraphs (central points)
identical-sounding words, *see* homophones

introductory phrases, 8–9,
    47–8
'it's' and 'its', 34

key points
    how to emphasise, 76–80
    in introductions, 90
    see also paragraphs
        (central points)

linking ideas, see flow
'linking words and phrases'
    examples of, 96–8
    over-reliance on, 55
    at start of paragraphs, 55

main clauses, definition of, 3
main points, see key points;
    paragraphs (central
    points)
meaningless words and
    phrases, 94
muddled thinking, 63, 93

organisation

of ideas into paragraphs,
    51–2

paragraphs, 51–62
    central points, 52, 56, 59
    content of, 52–3
    a formula for construction
        of, 53–4
    links between, 55, 96–8
    main points, see
        paragraphs (central
        points)
    proofreading for clarity
        of, 56
    purpose of, 51
    pyramid structure, 53
    topics, 59; see also topic
        sentences
parallel sentence structure,
    74–5
past participles, 41
personal opinion, see 'I'
phrasing
    useful phrases for essay
        writing, 96–8

possessive pronouns (yours,
        hers etc.)
    and apostrophes, 33, 36
present participles (-ing
        words), 41, 66
punctuation, 1–37
    see also apostrophes;
        bullet points;
        colons; commas;
        full stops;
        semicolons

quotations
    phrases to introduce, 97
    punctuation of, 11–12,
        20–1
    resuming an argument
        after, 97

reading out loud, 42, 45, 48,
        49, 93
relative pronouns (who, that,
        which etc.), 65, 70
role play, 93

semicolons, 3, 24, 25–9
  confusion with colon, 24
  main uses, 26–9
  proofreading for, 29
sentences, 39–49, 63–80
  breaking into smaller
      units, 65–7
  clarifying structure of,
      46–9, 63–4, 74–5
  controlling syntax in,
      63–70, 81–5
  definition of, 39, 40
  fragments, 43–5
  incomplete, 40, 43
  proofreading for clarity
      of, 49
  punctuation of, 42
  'run-on', 1–3
  'standard sentence
      tester', 42
  strongest part of, 76–80
'springboard comments',
      53, 54
stem statements, 72–3
style, 63–91

see also concision; flow;
      key points; parallel
      sentence structure;
      sentences; syntax;
      word choice
subject (of a sentence), 39,
      40, 41, 46, 47, 48, 49
  definition and purpose of,
      40, 46
  starting with (to improve
      clarity), 47–8, 85
syntax
  controlling longer
      sentences, 63–70
  parallel sentence
      structure, 74–5
  untangling awkward
      syntax, 64, 81–5
  use of 'I' to simplify, 88

'therefore', 27, 29,
topic sentences, 53, 54,
      57–62
  formula for writing, 61
  proofreading for, 62

verbs
  finite, 40, 41
  main, 46, 48, 49
  non-finite, 41
  tense, 40

word choice
  deleting meaningless
      words, 94
  introducing variety, 94
  keeping it clear, vii, 81, 94